Pra
Healing
Body and Soul

Sally Macke

Liguori

Imprimi Potest: Thomas D. Picton, CSsR
Provincial, Denver Province, the Redemptorists

Published by Liguori Publications, Liguori, MO 63057
To order, call 800-325-9521, or visit Liguori.org.

Copyright © 2011 Sally Macke

ISBN 978-0-7648-2005-2

All rights reserved. No part of this publication may be reproduced, stored in a retrieval system, or transmitted in any form or by any means—electronic, mechanical, photocopy, recording, or any other—except for brief quotations in printed reviews, without the prior written permission of Liguori Publications.

Scripture citations are taken from the *New Revised Standard Version* of the Bible, copyright 1989 by the Division of Christian Eduction of the National Council of Churches of Christ in the USA. All rights reserved. Used with permission.

Liguori Publications, a nonprofit corporation, is an apostolate of the Redemptorists. To learn more about the Redemptorists, visit Redemptorists.com.

Cover design: Wendy Barnes • Cover image: Shutterstock

Printed in the United States of America
26 25 24 23 22 / 8 7 6 5 4

Introduction

This pamphlet is dedicated to all the patients I've had the privilege to listen to in my years as a hospital chaplain. They have powerfully witnessed to the strength of the human spirit, and I am grateful for their trust in me. I have tried to incorporate their common struggles into my prayers.

I believe the healing process is a partnership between our human efforts and the providence of our gracious God. So many patients have told me how important prayer was to them in their recovery process. I hope this pamphlet helps lead other patients, both inside and outside the hospital, to prayer and healing.

Loneliness

*"Turn to me and be gracious to me,
for I am lonely and afflicted."*
PSALM 25:16

I am alone, grappling with my sickness in this strange environment. Its sights and sounds are foreign to me, and my hospital bed is nowhere as comfortable as my bed at home.

I feel so lonely.

But you, O Lord, are as close to me as the air I breathe. I am never alone, for you are with me always.

I turn to you, Lord, in my loneliness. In your love and compassion, show me your presence.

With you by my side, I can face anything. With you in my heart, I can find rest, assured of your love.

Let my heart find its home in you, and only in you.

Remaining Hopeful

"Happy are those whose help is the God of Jacob, whose hope is in the LORD their God."
PSALM 146:5

I am so uncertain about the future and I am starting to lose hope. I don't know what's going to happen, and the medical staff, though caring, cannot give me the assurance I need.

But you are a God of hope. You are a God who promises only goodness. You are a God who wants life for me and for all your creation.

I turn to you, Lord, with my questions and fears, and ask that you fill me with hope. Help me to trust in your love so that I can face the future with peace.

Give my family, too, the hope that they need, so that together we can rest in the arms of your love.

Prayer Before Surgery

*"You are my hiding-place and my shield;
I hope in your word."*
PSALM 119:114

Lord, I ask for your protection before my operation. I am anxious and fearful, but I pray for the grace to trust in you.

Bless my surgeon and the operating team. I thank you for their skill and knowledge, and for bringing me to them in my time of need. Fill them with your wisdom and guidance as they perform my surgery.

If it be your will, Lord, I ask that my surgery be successful, but give me the ability to accept whatever may happen, knowing you are with me always.

You are the Divine Physician, and I place myself in your care.

I Am Weary

*"At an acceptable time, O God,
in the abundance of your steadfast love,
answer me."*
PSALM 69:13

I am tired of this illness, and I long for easy solutions. Yet it seems that those solutions evade me.

Be with me, God, in my weariness. Be a stronghold for me as I face this new challenge. Let me know you are with me and you will never leave me to face my burdens alone.

I ask for your guidance as I face the decisions that await me. I ask for the best outcome to this situation, you who are my shield.

Give me the strength to welcome the future, secure in the knowledge of your love for me. With your wisdom, make straight my path.

Confronting Pain

*"Hear my cry, O LORD; let my cry come to you.
Do not hide your face from me
in the day of my distress."*
PSALM 102:1–2

I hurt. All I can think about is my pain. I am engulfed in pain, and I can't take it much longer.

Jesus, you were nailed to a tree; you know what it's like to be in pain. You know my misery, and I believe you long to take it away from me.

God, if it be your will, take away my pain, but if not, be with me in my suffering. Wrap your loving arms around me and help ease my burden.

In the Garden of Gethsemane, Jesus, the Father gave you the strength you needed. I beg you to do the same for me.

Feeling Helpless

*"Do not cast me off, do not forsake me,
O God of my salvation!"*
PSALM 27:9B

I am a grownup, yet in this hospital environment, I have been made small. I cannot get out of bed, I cannot eat when I want, and I have to ask for medication when I need it. I am at the mercy of others.

I don't like feeling helpless. I don't like having to rely on others. I don't like feeling insecure about my future.

Be with me in my helplessness, God of my salvation. Show me my dignity in the face of my vulnerability, for I find this situation difficult.

Though I am not a child, I am *your* child. Give me your grace so I can accept my dependence on others, however long it may last.

A Prayer of Gratitude

*"I will thank you forever,
because of what you have done."*
PSALM 52:9A

I turned to you, Lord, and you answered me. Though I was fearful, you came to my aid. You showed me you are a God of goodness.

You are bringing about healing in my body, and I thank you. Because of you, I am getting stronger and more whole.

You have provided for me, and I feel so very blessed. You are a God who keeps your promises. How grateful I am for all you have done for me! I am filled with joy because of your care for me.

I know that I could not have made it without your help. With gratitude, I praise your name, and I will trust in you always.

Show Me Your Everlasting Faithfulness

> *"Satisfy us in the morning
> with your steadfast love,
> so that we may rejoice and
> be glad all our days."*
> PSALM 90:14

I feel like a boat without an anchor that is drifting out to sea.

I reach out for comfort, and though my family tries to reassure me, I feel lost. I long for home and my own surroundings.

I need you now, Lord. I need to know I can count on you. You have been there for me in the past, and I ask for your faithfulness to me again.

Help me understand you are a God who keeps your promises. I am one drop in the ocean of humanity, but I know you care for me and will not leave me.

Missing the Comforts of Home

*"The L<small>ORD</small> is my rock, my fortress,
and my deliverer, my God,
my rock in whom I take refuge."*
P<small>SALM</small> 18:2<small>A</small>

Whoever said one could rest in a hospital?

I'm tired, and I can't get comfortable in this bed. It is too noisy here to sleep. Just when I think I am drifting off to slumber, I wake up.

I don't want to be here. I wish I were home. I want to be in the safety of my own environment. I miss being surrounded by things that are lovingly familiar to me.

Surround me, Lord, with your comfort and your peace, so that I may rest secure, despite my discomfort. Show me your loving presence so I will feel safe and at home, no matter where I rest.

When I Need Wisdom

*"Make me to know your ways, O LORD;
teach me your paths.
Lead me in your truth, and teach me."*
PSALM 25:4–5A

There are so many options from which to choose, I am overwhelmed.

I have important decisions to make, and the way to proceed is not clear to me. I need your guidance, Lord.

Though my doctor is kind and informative, I know my body better than anyone else—anyone except you, God. You can lead me to the decision that is best for me.

You are a God of wisdom whose knowledge knows no bounds. You who created me, help me to care for your creation, my body, by leading me to the right decision.

Overcome by Exhaustion

*"O LORD, God of my salvation,
when, at night, I cry out in your presence,
let my prayer come before you."*
PSALM 88:1–2A

Sometimes I feel I can't go on. I am weary, overcome by exhaustion, so tired I could cry.

Where is the goodness I know is present in this situation? Am I just too blind to see it, Lord?

Infuse my being with your strength, God. Empower me with your determination so that I can go forward.

Help me to find the rest I need, so that I can feel refreshed in mind and spirit. Give me a better tomorrow, I beg of you.

I need you to carry me now, Lord, on the wings of your love, for this journey is too daunting for me alone.

Where Can I Find Joy?

> *"O God, you are my God,*
> *I seek you, my soul thirsts for you;*
> *my flesh faints for you."*
> PSALM 63:1A

I miss the laughter I had before this illness. I am a person who enjoys life, who loves to have fun. My world seems to have narrowed to the confines of this hospital room. Being here is no fun.

A pleasant smile, a friendly hello, these are all I need to find joy nowadays.

Please put people in my path who will lift me up so that I do not sink into desolation. Likewise, help me be pleasant, so that I can inspire others with your joy.

Lord, give me eyes to see and ears to hear whatever is beautiful, so that my spirit can sing again to the song of life.

Calm My Fears

*"Even though I walk through the darkest valley,
I fear no evil; for you are with me."*
PSALM 23:4A

I am frightened. I do not understand everything that is happening to me, and I need you, Lord. I am afraid of what lies ahead.

Try as I might, my mind keeps spinning with the possibilities of what could be. I cannot quiet my fears; they are too strong.

Help me, God, to see my situation realistically, so that I can think clearly. Take away the fear that threatens to tighten its grip on my very being.

You promised to always be with us, Lord, in the midst of our troubles. Let me know that with you by my side, I have no need to fear. Be my rock and my fortress, Lord.

Prayer for Steadfastness

*"Keep my steps steady
according to your promise,
and never let iniquity
have dominion over me."*
PSALM 119:133

I did not know this healing process would be so challenging. I am eager to be better but know it will take time. My thoughts are scattered and I am distracted.

I need your hand to steady me, Lord; I need you to keep me focused as I recover.

Help me stay on the course of action my doctor has outlined for me, Lord. I need to keep in mind what we are trying to accomplish: my healing.

Let me believe in my recovery. Show me I am making progress so that I will feel encouraged. Be a mighty oak to steady me; I am a sapling that bends with the wind.

Missing My Loved Ones

*"For I am poor and needy,
and my heart is pierced within me."*
Psalm 109:22

I do not know anyone in this hospital, and my family is unable to be here with me right now. I feel their absence keenly, and I miss them dreadfully.

My loved ones are a gift from you, God—they are a primary way you show me you love me. I wish they were here. I need them.

Help me to stay strong until my family can be with me again. Let me look to you, a wellspring in my heart, to bring me comfort and peace, now and always.

Be my mother and my father, Lord, my sister and my brother. Let your love, more powerful than any human love, fill my heart and bring me peace.

Why Now?

*"Out of the depths I cry to you, O LORD.
LORD, hear my voice!"*
PSALM 130:1

This is a bad time for me to be sick. I have so much going on in my life, and this illness is a huge inconvenience. Why did you allow me to be sick now, Lord?

I cannot stop thinking about all I have to do. My head is swimming with the unfinished details of my work, and with promises and appointments I haven't kept. I feel frustrated that my illness keeps me from doing what I need to do.

There must be a lesson somewhere in this experience, but I cannot see it now. Rein in my impatience at my loss of control, Lord, and give me the grace to accept my situation.

Communion of Saints

"Come, bless the L<small>ORD</small>,
all you servants of the L<small>ORD</small>,
who stand by night in the house of the L<small>ORD</small>!"
P<small>SALM</small> 134:1

There are holy people who have gone before me who show me the way to live. These people, your saints, inspire me by their trust in you and their love for others.

Among your saints are those who loved me and who have gone before me. I know that they are with you now, Lord, and continue to pray for me as well.

What a gift it is, Lord, that I can call upon them to help us in our life's journey!

I thank you for the communion of saints, who teach me the power of your love.

Still My Mind

*"You desire truth in the inward being;
therefore teach me wisdom
in my secret heart."*
PSALM 51:6

I need to still my mind, Lord. It buzzes with a million different thoughts, all competing for attention.

I feel betrayed by my body, by this illness. How could I have ended up in the hospital?

This place, with its stark efficiency and bustling staff, is like a dream. I feel lost and confused.

You are my shepherd, Lord, and I am one of your sheep. You care for me, you watch over me, and you will never abandon me.

Help me trust in your providence, and give me a share of your strength. Quiet my mind and my heart so I can hear your message of love.

Give Me Patience

*"Wait for the L*ORD*; be strong,
and let your heart take courage;
wait for the L*ORD*!"*
PSALM 27:14

Oh, I so long to be well. How I would love to feel good again and do the things I enjoy! The hours slowly tick by, and it feels like it's taking forever for me to recover.

I try not to bristle with irritation at the staff, but it's hard. They don't know what it feels like to be stuck in this bed. Help me to be pleasant, Lord, for they are just trying to do their job.

God, I need your patience. I need to remember that my healing is taking place in your time and not on my schedule. Help me believe that even now you are working to bring about greater strength within me.

Restore My Health

*"Incline your ear to me;
answer me speedily in the day when I call."*
PSALM 102:2B

This hospital staff is good, and I am working hard, too, Lord, to get better, but ultimately, I am in your hands. You are the one I count on to heal me.

I pray that you restore all the cells of my body to their original health. Surround me, from the top of my head to the tips of my toes, with your light and your love.

If it be your will, Lord, I ask that you heal me quickly, and give me acceptance and peace as I wait for you to do your work.

May your Holy Spirit infuse my whole being with the power of your resurrection, so that your love will triumph over my illness.

For the Hospital Staff

*"All your works shall give thanks to you,
O LORD, and all your faithful shall bless you."*
PSALM 145:10

I am so grateful for the care I am receiving in this hospital. The staff is caring and good.

Everyone is so busy, and I can tell they feel stretched by their workload. Please help their days go smoothly and give them joyful hearts as they do your work.

Let the medical staff look to you, God, for their well-being and their strength. Their work is not easy, and they need your assistance as they care for all the patients.

Please bless every person who works here, Lord, so they will know your love and be guided by your Spirit. Help them remember they are instruments of your healing and compassion.

Bless the Other Patients

*"But let all who take refuge in you rejoice;
let them ever sing for joy.
Spread your protection over them."*
PSALM 5:11A

I see suffering when I look around me, Lord. Many of the patients here are struggling and need your sustenance. I believe you suffer along with us, Lord, and want to bring us wholeness and fullness of life.

Your graciousness knows no bounds. You are a God of mercy and compassion. Show your people the strength of your care for them, Lord.

Help all the patients here know you are with them, and bring healing to their bodies now and in the future. May they be enlivened by your courage and consoled by your peace. Give them the grace to trust in you, Lord, for without you, we are nothing.

You Can Move Mountains

*"O L̲ord my God, you are very great.
You are clothed with honor and majesty."*
PSALM 104:1B

I have not heard any good news lately about my illness and recovery. If something could go wrong, it has. Everywhere I turn, there are problems to be solved, obstacles to be overcome.

But you, O God, are more powerful than any difficulty. You can make a way where there is no way. Your strength is mighty, your faithfulness is ever present.

I put myself into your hands, Lord, and ask that you reveal a solution where there seems to be none. Simplify my life, open wide the door to possibilities, and give me the faith to let go.

God, help me believe in your ability to do all things.

Dealing With Boredom

*"Evening and morning and at noon
I utter my complaint and moan."*
PSALM 55:17A

Trapped in this hospital room, the TV my only diversion, I am bored beyond belief. The hours, the minutes, drag by ever so slowly.

I feel so useless here. I wish I had something to do to pass the time, but nothing holds my interest. It's hard to concentrate, even on the things that I usually love.

If it is your will, help me get out of here soon, Lord. This is not how I want to spend my time, waiting, always waiting.

Uphold me by your strength, God, so I can persevere in the midst of this endless boredom. Give me the hope of a brighter tomorrow and the patience to deal with today.

A Plea for Peace and Quiet

*"I implore your favor with all my heart;
be gracious to me according to your promise."*
PSALM 119:58

It is so noisy here I do not think I can stand it. Conversations in the hallway, visitors, phone calls and the TV all serve to keep me irritable and awake. I need some peace and quiet.

I wish I were on a desert island, with only the sun and the sand to keep me company. The constant stimulation of this hospital environment makes me jumpy and on edge.

Lord, even if I cannot shut out the outside noise, bring stillness to my mind so I know you are here. Help me look for the ways you are present so I feel renewed by your Spirit.

Walk with me on this strange journey and give me peace.

I Need a Little Sunshine

*"Gladden the soul of your servant,
for to you, O LORD,
I lift up my soul."*
PSALM 86:4

I feel trapped within the four walls of my hospital room. I stare longingly at the trees outside my window and wish I could go outside and play.

I need a little sunshine, Lord. I need the restfulness of your creation to give solace to my spirit.

Create within my mind an oasis of beauty. Lead me to memories of lovely places I have been that still my soul and remind me of your presence.

The harsh fluorescent lights cannot compare to the glory of your sun, God. I appreciate the goodness of your earth so much more now.

Help me remember that soon I will be free to enjoy the beauty of your creation.

Health on the Horizon

*"I shall not die, but I shall live,
and recount the deeds of the LORD."*
PSALM 118:17

My journey toward healing has begun, and I look to the future expectantly. Everything is in place to assure my optimal health. I am excited to think I will get better soon!

Fill my body with the energy I need every day, and give me the stamina to keep going even when I may be tempted to falter.

I pray for the grace to maintain a positive attitude while I recover, Lord, and I ask that you keep me strong and determined as I mend.

Thank you for being my ally, God, as together we forge ahead toward my full recovery. Keep my resolve strong with your steadfast love so that soon I will be well.

Overcome by Self-Doubt

*"But you, O LORD, do not be far away!
O my help, come quickly to my aid!"*
PSALM 22:19

I'm worried I made the wrong decision about my plan of recovery. This hospitalization is much harder than I anticipated. There are so many problems I didn't foresee.

My mind keeps brooding over the options I considered before I came here, and I wonder if I should have taken a different course of action.

I turn to you, Lord, in my worry, and ask that you give me your peace that goes beyond all understanding.

Please show me whether I am on the right path, and if I'm not, please clarify for me which way I should go. Smooth away my fretfulness and help me abide in your love.

Why Is There Suffering, Lord?

*"Why, O LORD, do you stand far off?
Why do you hide yourself in times of trouble?"*
PSALM 10:1

I don't understand why I have to go through this. I rail against pain and the awful things that accompany being sick. I hate this illness.

You are a good and gracious God, and you made us in love, so why am I suffering, Lord?

I don't mean to be disrespectful. I don't want you to think I don't appreciate all the gifts you have given me, but it sure would help if I understood why there's so much agony in the world.

I know you have a plan for us all. Help me to trust in your plan.